MY BODY, MY RULES

I STAY SAFE

BY
LAYLA
OWENS

Enslow
PUBLISHING

Please visit our website, www.enslow.com.
For a free color catalog of all our high-quality books, call toll free 1-800-398-2504 or fax 1-877-980-4454.

Library of Congress Cataloging-in-Publication Data

Names: Owens, Layla, author.
Title: I stay safe / Layla Owens.
Description: Buffalo, NY : Enslow Publishing, [2026] | Series: My body, my rules | Includes index.
Identifiers: LCCN 2024054855 (print) | LCCN 2024054856 (ebook) | ISBN 9781978543867 (library binding) | ISBN 9781978543850 (paperback) | ISBN 9781978543874 (ebook)
Subjects: LCSH: Safety education–Juvenile literature. | Right to bodily autonomy–Juvenile literature.
Classification: LCC HQ770.7 .O94 2026 (print) | LCC HQ770.7 (ebook) | DDC 613.6–dc23/eng/20241226
C record available at https://lccn.loc.gov/2024054855
LC ebook record available at https://lccn.loc.gov/2024054856

Published in 2026 by
Enslow Publishing
2544 Clinton Street
Buffalo, NY 14224

Designer: Tanya Dellaccio Keeney
Editor: Caitie McAneney

Photo credits: Series art (notebook) Design PRESENT/Shutterstock.com; series art (stickers) tmn art/Shutterstock.com; cover Pixel-Shot/Shutterstock.com; p. 5 Tom Wang/Shutterstock.com; p. 7 Red Stock/Shutterstock.com; pp. 9, 17 fizkes/Shutterstock.com; p. 11 RyanJLane/iStock.com; p. 13 Krakenimages.com/Shutterstock.com; p. 15 komnphoto/Shutterstock.com; p. 19 Prostock-studio/Shutterstock.com; p. 21 PeopleImages.com - Yuri A/Shutterstock.com.

Printed in the United States of America

Some of the images in this book illustrate individuals who are models. The depictions do not imply actual situations or events.

CPSIA compliance information: Batch #CSENS26: For further information contact Enslow Publishing, at 1-800-398-2504.

CONTENTS

BOLDFACE WORDS APPEAR IN WORDS TO KNOW.

SAFETY FIRST

Your safety is important. You have the right to be safe from harm. It's helpful to know what you can do to keep your body and mind safe. Sometimes you might need to ask for help. Safety first!

YOU HAVE THE POWER TO KEEP YOURSELF SAFE.

TALK ABOUT IT!

You may get into a **situation** that doesn't feel safe. It might be new to you. You can talk about it with trusted adults in your safety circle. Ask what you should do. Get help. Your voice is an important tool.

YOUR SAFETY CIRCLE IS A GROUP OF THREE TO FIVE ADULTS YOU CAN TRUST. THEY MIGHT BE FAMILY MEMBERS, TEACHERS, OR COACHES.

SKY'S SAFETY CIRCLE

Sky needs help. A kid at school has been bullying her. He says mean things to her. He pushes her in the hallways. She's scared. She thinks about her safety circle: Mom, Uncle Kevin, and Coach Sarah. Sky tells Coach Sarah. She helps!

SARAH KNOWS SHE CAN REACH OUT TO ANYONE IN HER SAFETY CIRCLE FOR HELP.

STRANGERS

A stranger is someone you don't know. They aren't **connected** to you or your family. Some strangers are helpers. Others might make you feel **uncomfortable**. Never go with a stranger. Never take something from a strange adult. If they **insist**, ask someone for help.

POLICE OFFICERS ARE ONE KIND OF HELPFUL STRANGER.

STRANGE BEHAVIOR

Strange **behavior** is a good way to know if someone is safe or not. This behavior may even come from someone you know. They might ask you to keep a secret. They might touch you or say things that make you uncomfortable.

TELL SOMEONE IN YOUR SAFETY CIRCLE IF A PERSON MAKES YOU FEEL UNSAFE OR UNCOMFORTABLE.

THAT'S NOT SAFE!

Sometimes you might want to do things that aren't safe. You might want to jump from a tree if a friend does it. You might see unsafe objects, such as knives or fireworks, and want to try them. Keep away from danger—even if a friend **pressures** you to do it.

YOU MAY WANT TO SKATEBOARD WITHOUT A HELMET. BUT YOU NEED ONE TO KEEP YOUR HEAD SAFE.

FREYA'S FEELINGS MATTER

Sometimes, you might get a feeling something is just "not right." Freya was at her friend's house. Her friend's brother made jokes that didn't feel right. Her stomach started to hurt. She felt shaky. She listened to her feelings. She called her mom.

YOU CAN TELL SOMEONE IN YOUR SAFETY CIRCLE IF SOMETHING IS MAKING YOU FEEL UNCOMFORTABLE.

STAYING SAFE ONLINE

The internet can be a great tool. But not all of the internet is safe for kids. Never give your personal information to strangers online. Tell a trusted adult if a stranger tries to connect with you online.

PERSONAL INFORMATION INCLUDES YOUR NAME, WHERE YOU LIVE, AND WHAT SCHOOL YOU GO TO.

IT'S YOUR BODY!

You are the boss of your own body. You get to decide who you let close. You get to tell people when you feel uncomfortable. You get to make choices each day that can keep you safe. You have the power!

USE YOUR VOICE TO SPEAK UP ABOUT HOW YOU WANT TO BE TREATED.

WORDS TO KNOW

behavior: The way someone acts.

connected: Known or tied to. Connect may also mean to meet up.

insist: To make a demand.

pressure: To try to force someone to do something.

situation: Something that is happening.

uncomfortable: Uneasy.

FOR MORE INFORMATION

BOOKS

Catena, Melissa. *Stranger Safety*. Minneapolis, MN: Jump!, Inc., 2025.

Ganeri, Anita. *Body Privacy*. Buffalo, NY: The Rosen Publishing Group, 2025.

WEBSITES

Online Safety
kidshealth.org/en/kids/online-id.html
Learn more about online safety with this helpful KidsHealth website.

Safety Tips
www.safekids.org/big-kids
Review these safety tips with a parent or teacher to learn about how to stay safe in many sticky situations.

Publisher's note to educators and parents: Our editors have carefully reviewed these websites to ensure that they are suitable for students. Many websites change frequently, however, and we cannot guarantee that a site's future contents will continue to meet our high standards of quality and educational value. Be advised that students should be closely supervised whenever they access the internet.

INDEX